HOUGHTON FEAST

The Ancient Festival of Houghton-le-Spring

Best Wishes

Paul Lanagan

New Houghton Feast illuminations were unveiled at Houghton Feast 2000 as part of the special Millennium celebrations. Millennium events included a Flower Festival in the Church of St. Michael & All Angels, a Ken Richardson Heritage Exhibition, a Big Top Circus and a History of Houghton Pilgrimage.

Previous page: Houghton Feast hymn singing in the Coronation year of Her Majesty, Queen Elizabeth II, 1953. Note the ERII illumination in the background.

First published in 2002 by Paul Lanagan

Printed by The Gilpin Press
Pottery Yard
Houghton-le-Spring
DH4 4BA

ISBN 0 9543253 0 3

Contents

John Mawston, left, and Paul Lanagan (author) promoting the Houghton Feast book. [Photograph: Northeast Press Ltd., Sunderland Echo]

Foreword

It gives me immense pleasure to provide a few sentences of support for this book. I am delighted that such a young, enthusiastic author as Paul has chosen the traditional Festival of Houghton Feast for his first work. I do know that it was a labour of love and as a local lad, the annual Feast is very dear to his heart.

Indeed, the Feast has been the highlight of my almost fifty year career in Local Government. As Chairman of the Feast Steering Committee and Ward Councillor for Shiney Row, I have seen the Feast develop and change with the support and encouragement of Houghton Urban District Council and then the City of Sunderland Authority.

Houghton Feast is truly unique and each year involves more than thirty local community groups participating in over fifty different events and activities within the ten days of the Festival programme - where else could we see the range of fireworks to flower shows, church services to concerts, street theatre to road races and ox roast to fun fair? Houghton Feast has the lot and much more! The Festival gives Houghton-le-Spring and District some civic pride - and I'm proud to be associated with Houghton Feast and this book.

JOHN MAWSTON, JP, ISM
Chairman, Houghton Feast Steering Committee

Ron Young, left, and fellow Rotarian Derek Moss, at the Millennium traditional ox roasting.

Introduction

I first met Paul as a young lad when he appeared on the site of the traditional ox roast and asked questions and showed interest way beyond his years.

Since that time I know he has worked extremely hard and researched diligently for information from myself and many others to compile a history of this unique annual festival and is grateful for the reception and assistance he has been given by these people and associations involved in maintaining the Feast traditions.

I am pleased to see this dedication come to fruition in the form of this excellent book which I recommend to you, not only as an enjoyable read now but also with the hope that it becomes a ready reference in the future. I wish Paul every success and happiness in his chosen career, whatever direction it may take.

Enjoy the book!

RON YOUNG
Public Relations Officer & Ox Roast Co-ordinator
Rotary Club of Houghton-le-Spring

Acknowledgements

This book is dedicated to the late Ken Richardson with whom I found my inspiration and to the memory of Billy Purvis for making me laugh. I also pay tribute to the many people who give their time so generously in the organisation of Houghton Feast. My gratitude is given to my wife, Lyndsay, and my daughter, Adonia, for supporting me whilst researching for this book. My sincere thanks go to Lena Cooper for her help and encouragement and for reminding me that the glass is always half full and not half empty. I would also like to thank the following people and I apologise to anyone I may have missed:

Russ Addison; John Alevroyiannis; George Bennison; Geoffrey Berriman; Angela Bowler; Linda Bromfield; Andrew Clark; Linda Corfield; Pat Crawford; Cecil Clark; Val Craggs; Geordie Davison; Wendy Davison; Leanne Davison; Alan Dickinson; Brian Dodds; Louise Farthing; Frank Graham; Joe Hall; Ted Hall; Julia Hankin; George Henderson; Richard Higgins; Bob Horn; John Hunt; Robert & Angela Hunter; Fraser Kemp, M.P.; Joan Lauderdale; Jim Lawson; Teresa Legg; Robert Lloyd; B. McCaffery of Gateshead; Stuart McLaren; Sally Mitten; Derek Moss; John Murphy; Ken Murray; Jamie Naisbitt; George Peebles; Elizabeth Porter; Annie Pratt; Ian Price; John Price; Tom Purvis; E. Ralf of Washington; Kevin Reilly; Kayleigh Robertson; Ian Robinson; Alf Roxby; Wilf & Doreen Richardson; Anne Ridley; Janetta Scurfield; Charles Slater; Andrew Smith; Ashley Sutherland; Maureen Thompson; Dick & Marion Toy; Paul Wappat; Ian Warburton; Brenda Weatherburn; Sandra White; Anne Wilson; John Wood and John Wright.

This book would not have been possible without help from the following people:
John Mawston, J.P., I.S.M.; Ron Young; Rev. Ian Wallis; David Richardson; Alan Robinson and the Storehouse Pharmacy, West Rainton.

The co-operation and help of the following is also greatly appreciated:
The Sunderland Echo & Northeast Press Limited;
Beamish North of England Open Air Museum;
BBC Radio Newcastle;
The Evening Chronicle;
Sunderland Library Local Studies Section;
Newcastle City Library Local Studies Section;
Tyne & Wear Archives Service;
Tyne & Wear County Museums;
Durham County Records Office;
Houghton-le-Spring & District Local History Group.

CHAPTER 1

BERNARD GILPIN AND THE ORIGINS OF HOUGHTON FEAST

It is often said that Bernard Gilpin, Rector of Houghton-le-Spring 1557 - 1583, was the originator of Houghton Feast but it is more likely that the Feast started in the 1100s as Michaelmas - the festival of the dedication of the Parish Church of St. Michael and All Angels. Another misconception about the Feast's origin is that the Feast was a celebration of Gilpin's safe return to Houghton after his arrest for heresy when the country was under the rule of Mary I.

A possible origin is suggested in the History of Durham 1894 by Francis Whellan & Co.:

Houghton Feast is held annually on Monday after Michaelmas day. The festival is continued with great spirit for three or four days, during which period there are horse-races and various other amusements. The origin of country feasts or wakes, which are usually observed on the Sunday next after the saint day to whom the parish church is dedicated, took their rise from a letter written by St. Gregory the Great to Melitus Abbot in these words, "It may therefore be permitted them, that on the dedication day, or other solemn days of martyrs, they make themselves bowers about their churches, and refreshing themselves and feasting together after a good religious sort, kill their oxen now to the praise of God and increase of charity, which before they were wont to sacrifice to the devil," - Bede's "Ecclesiastical History".

Gilpin did, however, have an important role to play in the Feast's history when he would welcome and feed his parishioners and their families each Sunday from Michaelmas to Easter, and it is thought that he would regularly give a bullock or hog for roasting to feed the Parish's poor.

The lineage of the Gilpin family. It was said in the Monthly Chronicle of North Country Love & Legend, 1887 that:

With Houghton-le-Spring the name of Bernard Gilpin will be ever associated; The 'Apostle of the North', has been often mentioned in connection with the annual and most ancient feast of Houghton. But Bernard Gilpin did not 'originate' Houghton Feast as has been but recently repeated.

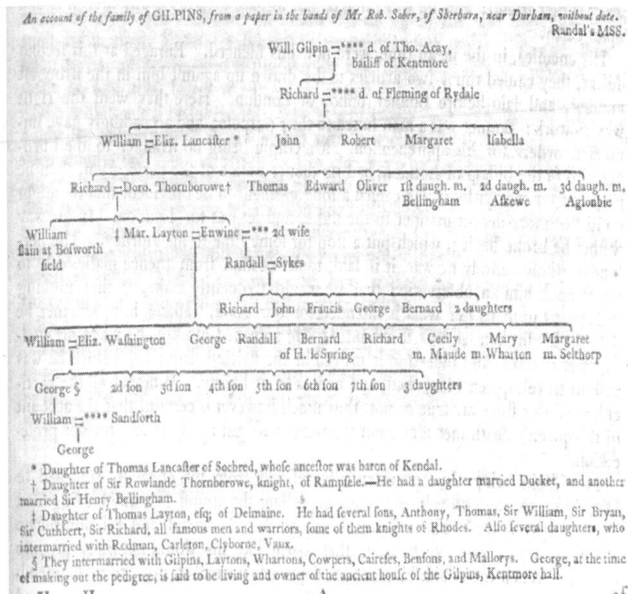

An account of the family of GILPINS, *from a paper in the hands of Mr Rob. Saber, of Sherburn, near Durham, without date.*
Randal's MSS.

Will. Gilpin = **** d. of Tho. Acay, bailiff of Kentmore

Richard = **** d. of Fleming of Rydale

William = Eliz. Lancaſter * | John | Robert | Margaret | Iſabella

Richard = Doro. Thornborowe † | Thomas | Edward | Oliver | 1ſt daugh. m. Bellingham | 2d daugh. m. Aſkewe | 3d daugh. m. Aglonbie

William ſlain at Boſworth field | ‡ Mar. Layton = Enwine = *** 2d wife

Randall = Sykes

Richard | John | Francis | George | Bernard | 2 daughters

William = Eliz. Waſhington | George | Randall | Bernard of H. le Spring | Richard | Cecily m. Maude | Mary m. Wharton | Margaret m. Selthorp

George § | 2d ſon | 3d ſon | 4th ſon | 5th ſon | 6th ſon | 7th ſon | 3 daughters

William = **** Sandforth

George

* Daughter of Thomas Lancaſter of Sochred, whoſe anceſtor was baron of Kendal.

† Daughter of Sir Rowlande Thornborowe, knight, of Rampſele.—He had a daughter married Ducket, and another married Sir Henry Bellingham.

‡ Daughter of Thomas Layton, eſq; of Delmaine. He had ſeveral ſons, Anthony, Thomas, Sir William, Sir Bryan, Sir Cuthbert, Sir Richard, all famous men and warriors, ſome of them knights of Rhodes. Alſo ſeveral daughters, who intermarried with Redman, Carleton, Clyborne, Vaux.

§ They intermarried with Gilpins, Laytons, Whartons, Cowpers, Cairefes, Benſons, and Mallorys. George, at the time of making out the pedigree, is ſaid to be living and owner of the ancient houſe of the Gilpins, Kentmore hall.

VOL. II. 4 A of

"No mention of the Feast would be complete without paying tribute to my good friend John Mawston and his team, whose dedication make it the success it is."

Fraser Kemp, M.P., 2002

Bernard Gilpin's tomb and the Houghton Well Dressing in 2001.

In Feast years gone by, the Church jewels would be on display here and the tomb would also be decorated with evergreens.

In 1583 Gilpin was knocked down by an ox in Durham Market Place and died shortly afterwards.

A stained glass window in St. Michael's Church, featuring Bernard Gilpin.

The Gilpin crest, shown at the foot of the window, consists of an oak tree piercing a boar and has become the symbol of Houghton Feast (see page 2).

"Houghton Feast is a fantastic week of events."

Cllr Ken Murray, 2001

A re-creation of Gilpin's crest by local florist Brenda Weatherburn. The display took ten hours to make and the flowers lasted almost two weeks.

[Photograph: Northeast Press Ltd., Sunderland Echo]

"It was a great privilege to be part of a special unique Millennium attraction at Houghton Feast. We tried to work with the grain of the Church so to enhance its inherent beauty and to emphasize features, which are significant with the history of Houghton and my interpretation of the Millennium prayer."

Brenda Weatherburn, 2002

A closer view of Gilpin's tomb in the South transept of St. Michael's Church.

The inscription on the tomb reads: 'Bernard Gilpin. Rector of this church, died on the 4th day of March in the year of our Lord 1583'.

Another view of Gilpin's crest in St. Michael's Church as part of the Houghton Feast Millennium celebrations.

Heather Yule, a Celtic harpist and storyteller, at the Celebrity Concert in St. Michael's Church. The use of the Church for concerts and the like is a relatively new concept, introduced during Rector Noel Gwilliam's time at Houghton.

A small child taking time out from the fun of the fair to view the floral art in St. Michael's Church.

A rare interior view of the Houghton Feast Church Service at St. Michael & All Angels' Church, October 9th, 1960. Where are the people pictured now?

St. Michael's Church during the musical extravaganza 'Jonah and the Whale', as performed by Church members at Houghton Feast 2000.

Children entering St. Michael's Church at Houghton Feast time, *circa* 1930. The Church has always been at the heart of the Feast.

Guests at the 1997 Festival Civic Service. Seen here in the grounds of St. Michael's Church are, from left: The Mayor of Sunderland; the Mayoress; the High Sheriff of Tyne & Wear, Mrs S. Murray; Mr Murray; Father W. O'Gorman and Rector Ian Wallis.

Welcome to

HOUGHTON FEAST

SUNDAY, OCTOBER 8th 1967

"This is the Day that the Lord hath made;
We will rejoice and be glad in it".

**EXHIBITIONS IN CHURCH AND KEPIER
THROUGHOUT THE FEAST**

A Houghton Feast leaflet from 1967. Such leaflets were used at Feasts in the early 1960s and were the forerunners to the more detailed Houghton Feast programmes. It was said in the Durham Advertiser newspaper at the time:

HOUGHTON FEAST, 1967 VERSION MADE HISTORY. Music and song, fun and frolic, sport and shows, ox-roasting and the gigantic carnival parade were the ingredients of the 1967 Houghton-le-Spring 'Feast' which will go down in history as one of the most memorable, and a forerunner to even greater festivals in the future.

Chapter 2

THE TRADITIONAL OX ROAST

The ox roasting ceremony has its origins way back in Elizabethan times when Bernard Gilpin started the tradition by roasting an ox or hog for the poor people of the Parish. The annual ox roasting tradition disappeared for many years until the 1960s but there are accounts of two ox roastings taking place before the revival, one in 1887 on the Golden Jubilee of Queen Victoria's accession to the throne, and another in 1896:

Above: A representation of what the ox roasting event could have looked like in years gone by. The artist was Robert Lowerson, who was well known for his cartoons in the Football Echo.

Eighty-year-old Mr Harry Fitton, of Gilpin Street, Houghton, recalls that it was around 1896 on a New Year's Day that a large white bullock was roasted in the Lake grounds. Mr Fitton was working as a butcher at the time and helped kill the beast. He recollects that disaster almost overtook the ceremony when the large wooden spit broke, and the carcase fell on to the open fire. Willing hands rushed to the rescue and the carcase was transferred to a large steel pole which was kept revolving over the fire by the turning of a cart wheel. He believes the animal was a gift to the town from a showman who attended Houghton Feast.

The Sunderland Echo, September 30 1954

Right: An artist's rendering of the traditional ox roasting, as featured in the 1987 Houghton Feast programme.

The ox roasting event is housed in the custom made tent on the corner of the Rectory field.

The generosity and competitive pricing by Sunderland Scaffolding is greatly appreciated.

In 1967 the Rotary Club of Houghton-le-Spring agreed on behalf of the newly formed Houghton Feast Steering Committee to revive the ox roasting tradition. Houghton butchers Jack Kinmond and Bill Curry, who had both roasted an ox at the nearby Lambton Park on the baptism of Viscount Lambton's son, were in charge of the event.

Nowadays, the ox roasting ceremony takes place on the Monday of the Feast week in a tent on the main corner of the Rectory field. Only once has it not happened when in 1996 the ox roasting equipment disappeared. Fortunately in 1997 a new spit was made by Alex Young, the man who had made the original.

The ox roasting equipment as made by Alex Young of CWR Fabrication, at a cost of almost £3000.

In 1967 the ox was cooked on an open fire of coke.

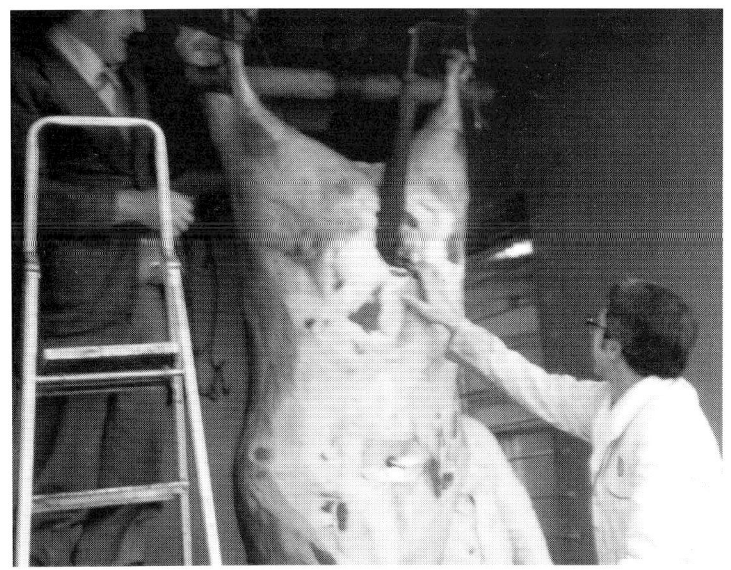

Preparation of the ox in the mid 1970s.

The immense size of the beast meant stepladders had to be used in the preparations.

The event is still organised by the Rotary Club of Houghton-le-Spring and involves a great deal of hard work by its members. The meat is prepared locally in Pipers Quality Butchers of Easington Lane. In the past a whole bullock was used but four large boneless joints of meat are now used, owing to the Government's ban on beef on the bone. The meat is attached to a spit in the shape of a beast, with clamps and wire strapping.

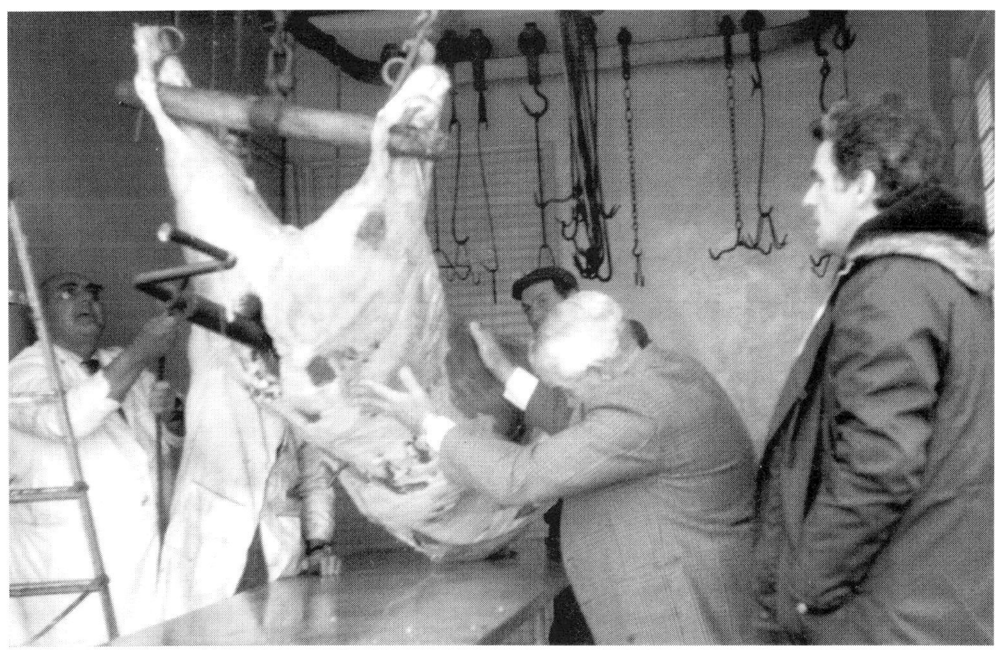

Further preparation of the ox. Driving the spit down the animal's spine was said to be backbreaking work.

Delivery of the ox to the tent on the Rectory field, 2001. It is wondered how the beast would have been transported in the time of Bernard Gilpin.

The enormous size of the ox meant that there was plenty of meat for sandwiches, as seen here in the 1970s. Even the dogs would get their share from the plentiful supply of bones.

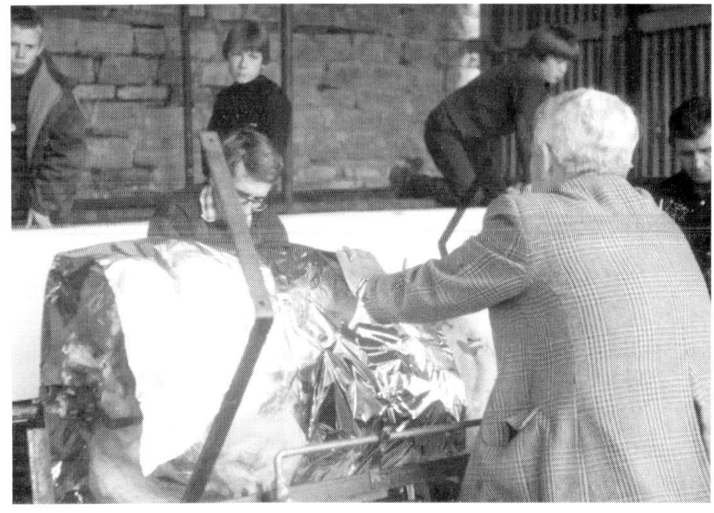

Another scene from the ox tent in the mid 1970s.

The ox is being wrapped in foil prior to roasting, by Walter Winship.

On Feast Sunday the equipment is brought to the tent and is assembled and connected to a gas supply. The heavy ox, which weighs several hundred pounds, is then delivered and lowered by crane onto the equipment and is covered in several layers of aluminium foil.

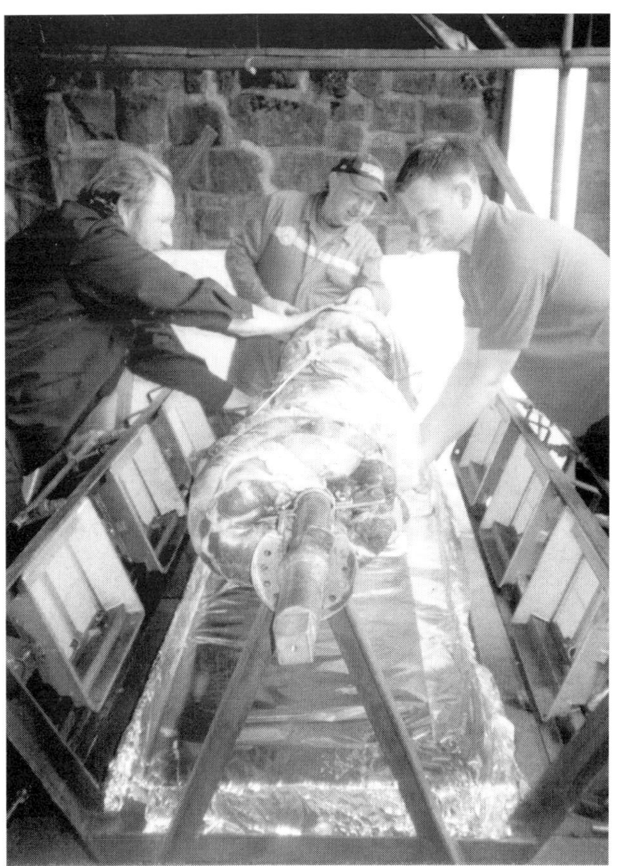

The six gas burners are lit and members of the Rotary Club keep a constant vigil on the ox, usually in two-hour sit-ins.

The ox used to be roasted for almost 24 hours but the boneless joints take a lot less time at approximately 18 hours. The Public Health department make regular checks before the meat is given the go-ahead for sale.

Houghton Rotarian, Alan Dickinson, making final preparations at the 2001 ox roasting event, with help from gasmen Ted Hall (left) and John Hunt (right).

Preparations in the ox roasting tent on the Rectory field. Ox roasting co-ordinator, Ron Young, can be seen on the left.

A cosy night at the ox roasting tent with Houghton Rotarians Derek Moss and Alan Dickinson (right).

Ashley Burland supervising the cooking ox on Feast Sunday night, 2001. Throughout the night, passers-by and the local police call into the tent to view the progress and give the Rotarians well wishes.

The ox cooking through the night of Feast Sunday.

October is a month well known for bad weather and the year 2000 was no exception. Heavy rain led to people having to queue in a deluge for an ox sandwich. For the first time in many years the event did not manage a complete sell out.

On Feast Monday, bread buns and gravy are brought from the local Edinburgh Bakery, ready for the sale of ox sandwiches. Members of the public start queuing several hours before the Mayor of Sunderland arrives to carve the first ox slice. Many hours are spent with the Rotary Club serving up around 1500 sandwiches, the proceeds of which go to local charities. The support of the public is greatly appreciated, as are the sponsorship and competitive pricing of the event's suppliers.

Mayor Ken Murray carving the first slice of ox at the 2001 ox roasting.

Derek Moss, left, lends a helping hand with freshly baked bread buns from the Edinburgh Bakery.

The annual ox roasting is a popular event of the Feast. The queue has been known to stretch down to the bottom of the Rectory field. Seen here in 1976 are, from left, Ron Young; Reg Harrison; George Bennison; Walter Winship; Mayor of Sunderland, Charles Slater; Bill Metcalf; Rector Peter Brett and Ron Hall.

[Photograph: Northeast Press Ltd., Sunderland Echo]

"There was a humorous incident at the ox roasting. Being of the Jewish faith I am not allowed to eat non-kosher food, particularly meat. The local vicar stood over me to make sure I did not commit a breach of the rules. I am bound to say that it looked so succulent that I was sorely tempted."

Memory from Charles Slater, Mayor of Sunderland 1976 - 1977

An outward view of the traditional ox roast event with co-ordinator Ron Young, and a hungry and wet crowd. The lady to the right of the crowd has regularly been first in the queue whatever the weather.

Left: Jack Kinmond presenting the first traditional ox roast sandwich to Rector Noel Gwilliam, Saturday, October 7th, 1967.

Below: Lyndsay Lanagan and her daughter, Adonia, with the first ox sandwich from the 33rd annual ox roasting event, Monday, October 8th, 2001.

[Photograph: Northeast Press Ltd., Sunderland Echo]

ROAST BEEF ON FEAST MENU

HOUGHTON Rotarians, roasting a whole ox for Houghton Feast, kept the spit turning throughout the night — and were still at it today, when the picture above was taken.

When the Feast opened last night with the switching on of the illuminations in the town, the ox was hoisted on to the spit in the Rectory Field in Dairy Lane and the fire started. It is hoped the ox will have cooked sufficiently to have sandwiches from it for festivities later today.

Coun. John Mawston, chairman of Houghton U.D.C., declared the Feast open and is see below about to throw th master switch to set the tow ablaze with colour.

This year several organization have joined forces with th Council to brighten up th Feast. —S.I

Left: The reporting of the revived ox roasting in the Sunderland Echo, October 7th 1967. The day of sale was a Saturday.

"The beast was suspended on a spit directly over a fire to roast. The fat from the ox fell into the fire causing a flare-up, incinerating it in a couple of hours. The organisers had to contact all the butchers in the area to get roast beef to put in the sandwiches!"

Memory from Russ Addison, 1960s

Below: A view of the revived ox roasting, with Councillor John Mawston turning the spit, in 1967. Back then, the ox sandwiches cost 1/6, about 7½ pence in today's money.

The cover of the 1976 Houghton Feast programme of events.

"The ox sandwich was very tasty and reminded me of historic links going back hundreds of years. I was amazed that hundreds of people queued in a deluge to purchase the ox sandwiches."

Memory from Cllr Brian Dodds, Mayor of Sunderland 2000 - 2001

CHAPTER 3

PEOPLE OF THE FEAST

Councillor John Mawston, Chairman of the Houghton Feast Steering Committee, right, with Mayor and Mayoress Gowan Scott.

John Mawston joined the Urban District Council in 1955 and has been associated with the Feast since then (see also page 46).

Oswald Noel Gwilliam, Rector of Houghton from 1948 to 1972, helped rejuvenate the Houghton Feast celebrations during his time at Houghton.

Rector Gwilliam initiated the outdoor community hymn singing event and dedicated a lot of time and effort to the revival of the Feast.

"We owe a lot to the vision of Oswald Noel Gwilliam."
Marion Toy, 2002

Members of the Urban District Council. Councillor John Mawston can be seen second row, second from right. The UDC was not fully responsible for the organisation of Houghton Feast until the late 1960s, when the Feast was greatly expanded.

The Houghton Feast Steering Committee meeting in Houghton Library, May 16th, 2002. The Committee comprises over thirty local groups and seen here are, from left: John Hodgson; Brian Coulson; Bob Heron,Ward Councillor; Joe Lawson, Ward Councillor; John Price, Festival Organiser and Project Manager from Community Services; John Mawston, Chairman; Marion Toy; Val Craggs, from Library & Arts Section; Elaine Mills; Dave Burke; Dick Toy; George Westgarth; Bill Barron and June Storey.

Peter Mackenzie was a well known Methodist Circuit Missionary and preacher. In 1896, a year after his death, a book was written about his life as a servant of Jesus Christ.

The following extract from **Peter Mackenzie - His Life & Labours** by Rev Joseph Dawson, tells of the unfortunate event which happened to him when he visited Houghton Feast in 1848:

I remember him relating to me how he went once to Houghton-le-Spring to enjoy what was called 'The Feast', a species of rustic fair and merrymaking held annually. He sported for the occasion a pair of white pantaloons, and what was his chagrin, on returning from the fair to the inn where he had stabled his donkey, to find saddle and bridle gone, and as if that were not enough provocation, the perverse animal had rolled itself vigorously in the mire of the inn yard, and was not fit to lay a hand upon.

White trousers and a mud-plastered donkey formed an incongruous combination, and the disgusted sportsman returned home with the conviction that the way of transgressors can not only be hard, but at times disagreeably soft. It was probably to this incident he alluded on his last visit to Haswell, when, in reply to one who was urging him to come to Houghton-le-Spring for a day, he answered playfully, "Nay, no more Houghtons for me! You behaved badly the last time I was at Houghton Feast. Somebody stole both my pad and bridle."

Above: A drawing of Billy Purvis as featured in the 1875 book. Billy died on December 16th 1853 and is buried at St. Hilda's Church in Hartlepool.

Left: The witty Billy Purvis, from the archives of Newcastle Libraries & Information Service.

Visitors to recent Feasts will recognise the showmen names of *Murphy, Noble* and *Turner* but one name not so easily recognisable is Purvis. Billy Purvis visited Houghton Feast during the 1800s and is more well known on Tyneside.

Billy made his first visit of over thirty to Houghton Feast in 1818. He had a popular show booth and was liked by many.

A book was published in 1875 called **The Extraordinary Life of Billy Purvis, the Eccentric, Witty, and Popular Showman: His Sayings and Doings** by T. Arthur. The book gives us a fascinating glimpse as to what Mr Purvis was like and, in particular, what his time at Houghton Feast was like:

Billy in full costume during one of his performances.

Passing on to Wark, Corbridge, and Newcastle, they reached Houghton-le-Spring in time for the October Feast.

On coming up to his usual stand he found it pre-occupied by Mr. James Scott of Newcastle, with a large and magnificent Theatrical Pavilion, which threw Billy's plain show completely in the shade. It was 6d. and 1s., double Billy's price, still he said, "Oh hinnies, awm fairly haggished; this chep will be sure to carry sway ower poor Billy." But Billy was wrong, he remained the star and favourite of the fair, and was patronised accordingly.

About nine o'clock the first night two "gentlemen," Dr. Bell, and Mr. Myers, a shopkeeper, mounted the stage as he was about to turn out the audience, and demanded ten shillings. Billy, looking at them, said "what for, then"? "Oh," replied one, "it is for the Racing Fund." Billy said "the Racing Fund! why, aw've been at Houghton mony a time, an' aw never paid ne ten shillings before; and what for should aw pay't noo," and turned to go into his crowded show, when one of them said "if the money was not paid his show would come down in quick sticks, that Mr. Scott paid it without a word, and I'll be d——d but you shall pay too; now its all nonsense refusing to pay, for pay you shall." Billy reasoned that his show was only half the size of Scott's, and if Scott paid ten shillings, he ought only to pay five. Going down the steps, they ordered the constable to carry them away, which he did, and in order to get the people out of the show he had to borrow Mr. Scotts steps.

Mr. Anderson, Bailie, told Purvis he had no right to pay anything, to demand the steps or apply to the magistrates. Giving the constable this information, showed him he was wrong, and he delivered up the steps, but Billy says, "I decline the honour of carrying them, saying - 'you carried them away, an' you'll just ha'e to carry them back, for aw's not gan' to de yor dirty wark.' Half-an-hour after two lads brought my steps, and I was all right as the mail."

"MUSHEE" TAKES HIS LIBERTY.

Billy was well known for his performing bear. It is possible that Billy brought his bear with him to the Feast in 1836 or 1837.

Unfortunately the bear attacked a young boy and had to be shot.

The second day of the feast was a very busy day with him, and a heavy shower coming on about 4 o' clock, which lasted some time, crowds fled from the races and went into his booth; and all went smoothly on till nearly 10 o' clock, when the two gentlemen (?) again made their appearance, demanding the five shillings he had agreed to give. "Why didn't you take it last night when I offered it? you cannot get it now, as the wife has taken away the money; but if you'll wait till I get this tilt off I'll get you the brass." "Oh!" said the Doctor, "we want the money and no d——d nonsense." "Well, gentlemen, aw'll bring ye the money, only tell me where to come te." They made no answer, but went down the steps, and I followed, as I wanted to settle matters, but it was no go. They threatened to pull my show to pieces, and I saw they were bent on mischief, indeed, they took hold of the shutters and used their strength to pull them down.

I stood on the lowest step of the ladder, and said "Gentlemen, if you attempt to do anything to my booth, I'll black some o' yor eyes." The assembled crowd laughed, and seemed to applaud my determination. Dr. Bell had a stout imitation bamboo stick in his hand, with a silver head, and he lifted it saying - "D—n you, if we cannot get the money from you, we'll pay it out of you," and he followed up his threat by aiming a blow at my head, which my shoulder received instead, breaking his stick by the blow, and knocking me off the steps. The people cried, "Shame, shame!" The Doctor was a person of some importance in the village, and though I had many well-wishers in the crowd, they did not like to interfere.

Another drawing of Billy performing one of his comedic acts.

It was a beautiful moonlight night, and as I mixed with the people, explaining circumstances to some, the Doctor spied me, followed and struck me again. I now appealed to the crowd, "Gentlemen, will you see me murdered?" The blow was repeated, when I turned upon him, and fetched him such a whap on one side of his head, and down he went like a pair of old boots. "Here, Mr. Purvis," shouted some one, "here's a man pulling down the show." I ran to the depredator, Myers, and soon laid him sprawling. The Doctor came to the rescue, and hit me again; I returned the compliment with thumping interest, and floored the bonesetter.

Myers now took his turn, and with a piece of shutter he had torn from the booth, rushed up to me, making a fierce blow at my sconce, which I evaded; wheeled in and sent him head over heels. The Doctor and his assistant lay on the ground for some time, and no one seemed inclined to lift them up; while an overman belonging to Hetton-le-Hole, and a shoemaker living in Newbottle Lane, came to my assistance, and got me away to a public-house with my clown's dress still on, and behaved to me very kindly; offering to be a witness of the ill treatment I had received, should the matter ever come before the Magistrates."

He left the Doctor minus three front teeth, and Myers with a fractured leg through a fall. He could not sleep with thinking about it, and rose early next morning, up with his booth and bid farewell to Houghton. He could really not blame himself for this affair, for as he says, "they brought it upon themselves, like Tommy Todd's pig, by going the wrong way." He was always a quiet man, and never used physical force unless driven to it. A great pity that such blackguards should hold places in townships.

"I was at the Feast only once and I know it was in 1937. My Mam and Dad started a business selling pies and peas from the house - small meat pies and mushy peas. We would get the meat (hoff) on Wednesday and my older sister and younger brother would help to cut it up whilst Dad would cook it in a large earthenware bowl in the oven, fuelled by the coal fire.

The cover of the 1987 Houghton Feast programme of events.

All day Thursday, Mam would be making pastry and lining the tins while Dad would be filling them and cooking the pies. We kids would help out when we came in from school. Dad thought it would be a good idea to sell some pies at Houghton Feast. So that week and through the weekend there was frenzied activity, at the end of which some four hundred pies were ready to go. Bright and early Monday morning two large clothes baskets were filled with pies. Dad hoisted one on his shoulder, the other had me on one handle and my cousin on the other and off we went to Houghton. When we arrived, Dad staked out his pitch alongside the other sideshows and told my cousin and me to go and look around. I remember seeing a man stripped to the waist with a crowd around him. Someone from the crowd took some chains and tied the man up and padlocked the chains. The man twisted and turned and went through all kinds of contortions and finally freed himself to applause and cash contributions from the crowd."

Memories from Robert Lloyd, 1937

Chapter 4

FAIRGROUNDS

The photographs in this chapter show the various fairground sites used for Houghton Feast from the late 1800s to the present day.

It is likely that the first fairs of Houghton Feast were held in the Market Place, the original settlement of Houghton, in the form of a market selling local produce. Entertainment probably consisted of dancing bears, street theatre and show booths.

By 1895, the fairground had spread to the Lake grounds and surrounding streets. Older readers will remember the many stalls which lined the streets from Nesham Place, down Church Street and along the Broadway, selling pies, mussels, cockles and pease pudding sandwiches. Some may even recall the rides situated on old Robinson Street (now the Co-op car park).

The town's redevelopments in 1967 saw the fairground switch to the present day site of the Rectory field. The festivities tended to last four days, starting on the Saturday and finishing on the Tuesday but the increasing content of the programme of events has meant that the Feast activities now usually cover ten days or more.

A rare view of the Lake site in 1882, a year after Joseph Coulson diverted the nearby Houghton burn into it.

The Lake was a popular resort but mill owners downstream were deprived of their water supply and started legal proceedings. By 1890, the Lake had been abandoned and was soon filled in by two showmen, the Robinson brothers, and used as a showground.

An early view of the fairground on the Lake site, *circa* 1895. The ride to the right appears to be a Waltzer.

[Taken from the book 'Houghton in Old Picture Postcards' by the late Ken Richardson, published by the European Library, Zaltbommel, The Netherlands.]

Another early view of the Lake fairground, *circa* 1895. The Houghton Enterprise Centre is now housed on this site on the aptly named Lake Road.

Hamilton's Ice Cream Stall, inside the Sunderland Street entrance to the Lake fairground, *circa* 1905.

A showman's caravan at the Lake fairground, *circa* 1912.

A view of the Lake fairground in the 1920s. Can any reader identify the structures in the foreground?

The Lake fairground in October 1949. John Murphy's Super Waltzer can be seen to the right of the photograph.

The setting up of the fairground was as much fun for the local children as the rides themselves as this photograph from the 1930s shows.

The fairground on the Lake site in full swing, *circa* 1930s. The site was last used as a fairground in 1967 when the redevelopment of Houghton and the A690 road scheme commenced.

Fairground stalls at the Lake site in the early 1960s. The writing on the carousel reads: 'Catering for all classes'.

The Lake fairground in 1963. Note the Shuggy Boats in the foreground of the picture. It is anticipated that vintage rides from the past fifty years will feature at Houghton Feast 2002 as part of the Golden Jubilee celebrations.

The Lake fairground in 1963. The gardens of the former Union Workhouse and Public Assistance Institution (Heath House) can be seen in the background.

"I can remember one year when too many shows turned up and they could not all fit onto the show field so some of them set up next to the old Rafters building. That year the place was jumping - it was one of the best Houghton Feasts! The best firework display had to be last year's. No expense was spared!"

Memory from Angela Bowler, 2002

This thrilling ride was known locally as the Big Boat. Note the riders holding on tightly, at the bottom of the photograph.

Illuminated side stalls at the Lake fairground in the 1960s. It is said that the fair would continue into the early hours of the morning.

A general view of the Lake fairground in 1963. Acquilla Toogood's Rock and Roll Waltzer can be seen in the centre of the photograph.

A general view of Houghton Feast from 1949. Notice the people on the ride in the foreground.

A thrilling ride at the Rectory field fairground, 2001. The ride made great use of smoke and strobe light effects.

The fairground in the Market Place, in 1908. Note the chimneys in the centre of the steam-powered rides. The proprietors of the nearby Jolly Farmers Inn (now the Spring Inn) would often let the showmen use the pub's facilities for washing.
[Taken from the book 'Houghton in Old Picture Postcards' by the late Ken Richardson, published by the European Library, Zaltbommel, The Netherlands.]

Houghton Feast at the Market Place in 1959. Between 1930 and 1940, confusion arose between Houghton Urban District Council and Durham County Council over the collection of tolls for the erection of stalls in the Market Place. The cost to Mr T. Murphy, Amusement Caterer, for the four day use of the Market Place in 1930 was £125.

Houghton Feast in 1959. It is wondered if the riders still enjoy the Waltzer today.

The first ride of the fairground in 2001. Pictured are some well-known names from the history of the Feast. From left are: John Murphy; Councillor John Mawston and Colin Noble. Mayor Ken Murray can be seen in the Waltzer car.

Eyes down for bingo . . .

. . . eyes up for the camera.

A view of the Rectory field fairground from the main entrance, prior to the opening night.

"We would go to The Lake first of all, which had stalls with funny hats, toffee apples and hot dogs, and then we'd go on the roundabouts, penny slots, darts, rifles, and side shows such as the bearded lady or the man with no head or the five legged goat. I remember the noise and smell of the generators. The tiresome part would be the number of old neighbours and friends my mother and grandmother would recognise and have to renew acquaintance with! I'd usually get bored and wander off and get lost! Then we'd continue into the Market Place where there were more stalls and roundabouts. The Shuggy Boats and Drive Your Own Cars were always down there and then we'd reluctantly walk down Church Street to try to get back on a bus to Fence Houses."

Memories from
Anne Wilson, 1946 - 1959

A night-time scene of the Rectory field fairground in the year 2000.

An amazing view of the Meteorite ride at Houghton Feast 2000. Riders are secured in cages around the perimeter of the ride before the ride starts spinning and rising up to almost ninety degrees.

Jemma Walls (left) and Leanne Davison taking a thrilling ride on the Ski Jump at Houghton Feast 2000.

A 'Hook-the-pocket-monster' side stall - a contemporary version of 'Hook-the-duck'.

"My grandfather attended Houghton Feast in the 1920s, at the Market Place. I personally attended the Lake site in 1948 with the Waltzer and have never missed a year since then. Memorable years are those with the mud."

John Murphy Snr., 2002

Children trying their luck on a side stall at Houghton Feast 2000.

The Rhythm Master ride at Houghton Feast 2000. The modern day rides are driven onto the field and assembled several days before the opening of the fairground. In the past, some larger rides would arrive via railway at Fence Houses station and be transported to Houghton.

A night time view of Keith Turner's Waltzer.

The Mayor of Sunderland, Councillor Ken Murray, meeting the invited children at the early opening of the fairground at Houghton Feast 2001.

"Houghton Feast Monday was a fantastic Monday - it was noted all over the country. I remember 'Peggy the High Diver' who would jump into a tank of water up at the Market Place. When I was about nine, my father had a coconut stall and I would pick the balls up for him. If any of the coconuts got cracked he would take them into the pub for the landlord."

Memories from John Wright, 1950s

Children - big and small - having fun on a merry-go-round.

A decorative merry-go-round for the children. The author remembers thoroughly enjoying this ride as a child!

Driving on the Dodgems at the Rectory field fairground, 2001.

"One of my favourite rides is the Waltzer. At night it is a mobile disco with all the lights and the smoke machine."

John Murphy Snr., 2002

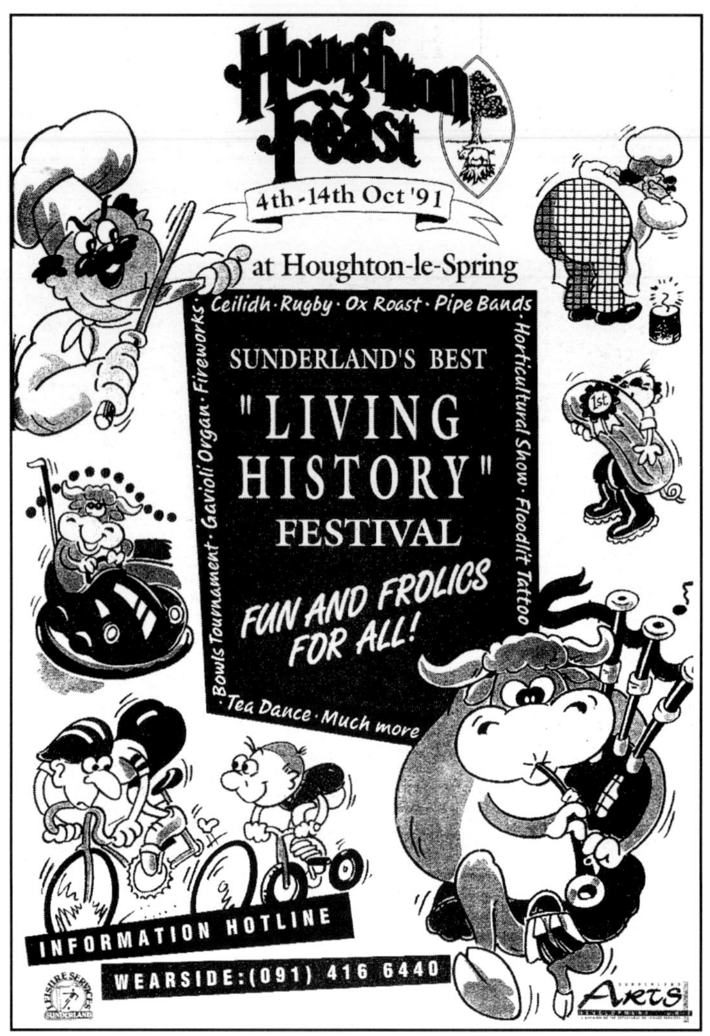

A poster from 1991 advertising Houghton Feast activities. Note that the Feast was supported by Sunderland Leisure Services.

"I remember the boxing booths. If you lasted three rounds with the boxer you would get paid a small fortune. I once saw a Danny Richardson from Hetton go the three rounds. Every Feast Monday, a bus load of what we called 'the Shields Wives' would spend the afternoon and night in the pubs of Houghton. In those days there was well over twenty pubs in Houghton! I can remember a fortune-teller called Gypsy Rose at the Lake fairground, and there was once a specialist act at the Market Place fairground. It was a European lady who balanced herself on a very high pole and would spin around on it. I can also remember the Wall of Death with the trick motorcyclists driving around it at full speed. There was also a lady at Houghton Feast who was covered from head to toe in tattoos."

Memories from Geordie Davison, 1940s - 1950s

CHAPTER 5

THE OPENING CEREMONY AND MILITARY TATTOO

The photographs in this chapter show scenes from various Houghton Feast opening ceremonies. The opening of the Festival takes place on Houghton Feast Friday and is the culmination of the Steering Committee's many months of careful planning.

The Broadway is filled with music and drama as members of the public, Civic guests and the Festival organisers gather in front of St. Michael's Church.

Each opening ceremony typically features the illuminations switch on and a military tattoo consisting of pipe bands and entertainers. The tattoo is organised by Houghton-le-Spring Pipe Band's representative, Kevin Reilly, and is concluded by a lone piper and bugler.

Houghton Feast in 1954. The immense crowd filled the entire Broadway.

Another view of the Broadway showing the military tattoo. The Broadway was filled with the sound of pipes and drums, as this photo from the year 2000 shows.

Houghton Feast crowds passing an illuminated White Lion pub in 1954. Houghton Feast attracts a large number of people into the town, with an estimated 65,000 people enjoying the various activities during the Festival's ten-day period.

Happy crowds at the opening ceremony and floodlit tattoo in 1996. The floodlit tattoo has been a customary part of the opening ceremony since 1985 and features pipe bands, military bands, drama and street entertainment, and concludes with a lone piper and bugler.

Houghton-le-Spring Pipe Band at the 1996 tattoo. Seen here are, from left: Andrew Givens; Kenny Shields; Ian Cruickshanks; Gordon Ross; Tommy Dobson; Les Givens; David Wheatley and Ian Logan.

Rob Durie, the bass drummer. Houghton-le-Spring Pipe Band has contributed to the Feast since 1981.

Another view of the Broadway at the opening ceremony in 1996. Like the Edinburgh tattoo, the ceremony goes ahead irrespective of the weather conditions.

Pipe bands at the Friday evening opening ceremony in 1996.

Mayor of Sunderland, Charles Slater, at the opening ceremony in 1976. Councillor John Mawston can be seen fifth from the left. The night of the opening ceremony was changed from the usual Friday to Thursday to accommodate Mayor Slater's Jewish faith. A firework display took place on the Friday.

The 1977 opening ceremony with Mayor Tom Bridges at the microphone and Rector Peter Brett in the foreground.

The illuminations switch on at the 2000 opening ceremony, with Mayor Brian Dodds, Mayoress Sylvia Dodds and Councillor John Mawston. The Mayor later said that he was worried that the lights might not have lit up but everything went according to plan when the new Millennium illuminations were unveiled.

The lighting of the Millennium beacon on the tower of St. Michael's Church in the year 2000.

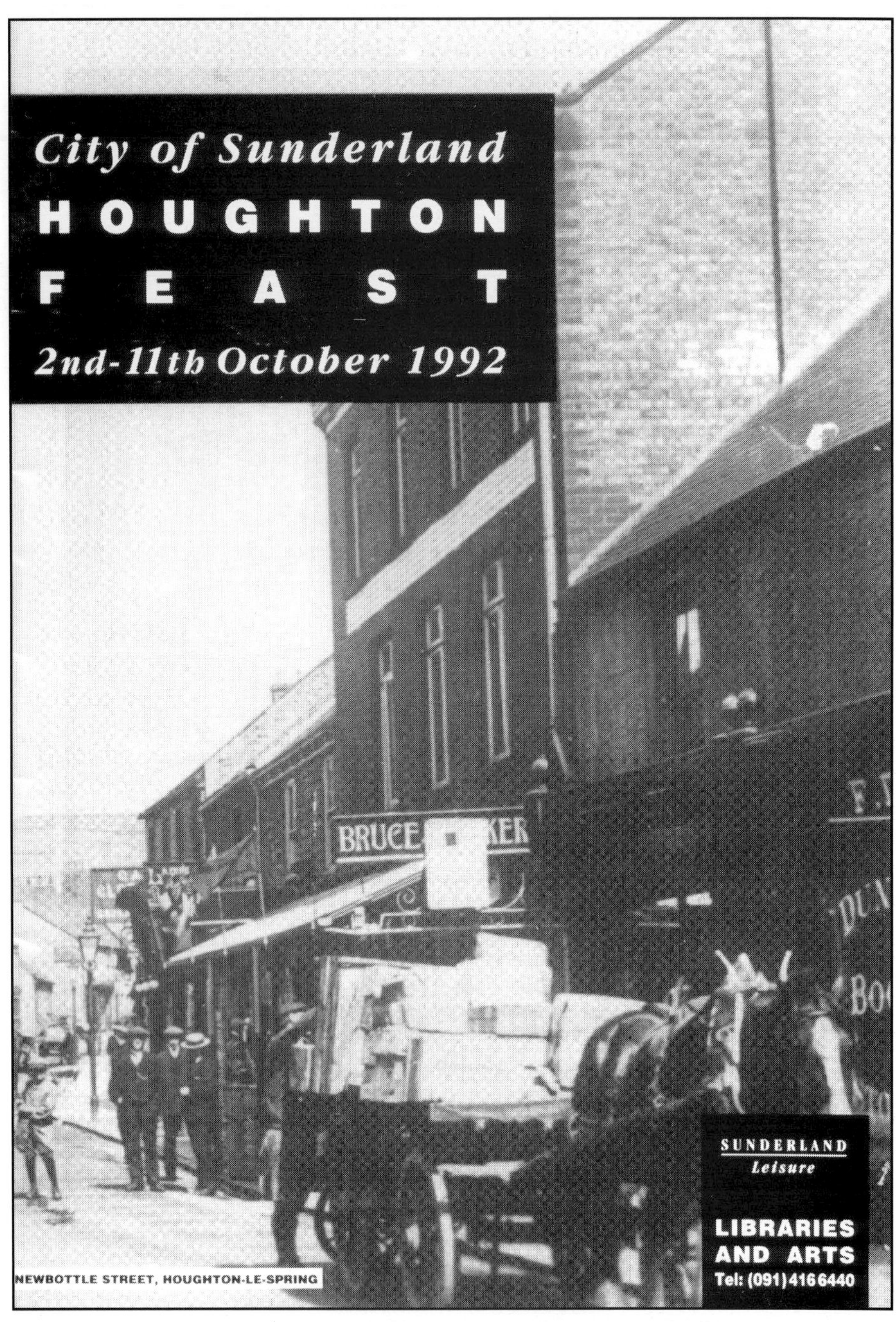

The cover of the 1992 Houghton Feast programme of events. Note at this time that Sunderland Leisure Libraries & Arts supported the Feast.

"In the 1970s my daughter, Helen, and I got our photo taken in front of the organ at Houghton Feast, by the local paper. We were quite surprised when the picture was used again in 1991. My daughter has never lived it down!"

Memory from Linda Corfield, 2000

CHAPTER 6

CARNIVAL PARADES

Throughout the years of World War II, most Feast activities were put on hold or greatly reduced, however the patronal festival of the Church was still celebrated with a military parade on Feast Sunday. The parades typically featured the Home Guards band, the Royal Tank Corps, police special constables, Civil Defence forces, Army cadets, Air Force cadets, Girls Training Corps and Girl Guides.

The carnival parade as we know it was introduced by the Round Table on Feast Saturday at the 1967 revival of Houghton Feast as a way of recapturing the spirit of pre-War Feasts when carnivals were a common sight throughout the year. It was described in the programme of events as *"a carnival of colour, fun, and spectacle, such as used to be held at the Feast in the 1930s"*.

The original route saw the carnival leave Burnside estate, proceeding along Station Road, through Newbottle Street and the Broadway, up Church Street and ending in the Market Place. Nowadays, the parade ends at Wheler Street.

The carnival parade is still a popular event with many thousands of spectators lining the route and the Round Table's en-route collection raises a substantial amount of money for local charities.

Fun at the Houghton Feast carnival parade. Pictured from left are Bill Smith; Ron Young pushing Ronnie Hall and Bill Shearer in the late 1960s.

"On Houghton Feast Saturday, my husband and I were busy judging the parade and didn't have time for a cup of tea. My husband always said that 'a hungry man will eat anything' and he was right; I was offered haggis for the first time and have loved it ever since!"

Memory from Annie Pratt, Mayor of Sunderland 1983 - 1984

Street theatre on Newbottle Street on Houghton Feast Saturday. Pictured on the left is Geordie Davison.

A float in the carnival parade in 1977. The Union flag and coins are in honour of the Queen's Silver Jubilee.

Carry on camping, on a float in the carnival parade.

The carnival parade in the 1970s. Age shall not weary them!

The same steam engine taking its place in the carnival parade of 2001.

Pipe bands in the 1977 parade, passing through Newbottle Street.

"The band became involved with the Feast in 1981. It started with a small solo piping competition held in Houghton Junior School."

Kevin Reilly, Houghton-le-Spring Band, 2002

A similar view of a pipe band on Newbottle Street. It was estimated by Northumbria Police that 10,000 spectators viewed the parade in 1997.

B. M. Stafford & Son's steam-powered vehicles are a regular sight at the carnival parade.

Another steam-powered vehicle, seen here at the 2001 carnival parade. Spectators on the White Lion public house roof can be seen to the right of the photograph.

Happy faces on Newbottle Street waiting for the carnival parade to pass, in the 1970s.

Civic guests judging the passing floats, in front of St. Michael's Church, 2001.

A Scout float in the parade at Houghton Feast in the 1970s.

Smiles all round on a float commemorating the Queen's Silver Jubilee in 1977.

A red, white and blue float celebrating the Queen's Silver Jubilee. This year's Feast will take the theme of the Golden Jubilee with many events reflecting the nostalgia of the past fifty years.

Another scene from a carnival parade in the 1970s. The revived parade of 1967 featured Herrington Military Band, jazz bands, decorated lorries, vintage cars, traction engines and people in fancy dress.

Fence Houses Sapphires marching in the 1976 parade. Where are the children pictured now?

Vintage cars taking part in the 1997 parade, next to Rectory Park. The parade had over fifty entries, each of which received a commemorative plaque from the Mayor of Sunderland.

A parade many miles away from Disney World, with Mickey and Minnie Mouse taking part.

"It is the main week of the year in my constituency diary - both the individual events themselves and the Church services which I attend. It is tremendous to see the community coming together and it is a fantastic opportunity to talk to people involved in every walk of local life."

Fraser Kemp, M.P., 2002

Spotty dogs in the Houghton Feast parade. The building in the background is the present day Rectory but was once the old Tithe Barn.

A local jazz band taking part in the 1976 parade on Feast Saturday. The White Lion pub can be seen in the background with lion intact.

"I still always remember the date of the Feast as being around October 6th as that was the birthday of my first love. I can also remember losing a shoe in the mud."

Memory from Anne Ridley

A scene from the 2000 parade at the Newbottle/Sunderland Street junction.

Another local Scout Group at Houghton Feast, 1976.

The American Civil War Society at Houghton Feast, 2001. The Society set up camp at Houghton Kepier School and provided drama throughout the Festival with its re-enactments. The firing of the cannons could be heard as far away as Fence Houses!

St. Michael & All Angels' Youth Club taking part in the parade in 1976. The people pictured probably take their own children to the Feast now.

"Houghton Feast is an invitation to celebrate community life."
Rev Ian Wallis, 2002

This fascinating float took part in the 1976 carnival parade and depicts the nursery rhyme, 'There Was An Old Lady Who Lived in a Shoe . . .'

Cleveland Pipe Band in the 2000 carnival parade. Seen here is Bill Brown, Pipe Major.

Another Pipe Band at the 2001 carnival parade.

A float in the Feast parade of 1976. If it wasn't for the house in the background, one could easily be forgiven for thinking that this picture dated from the sixteenth century.

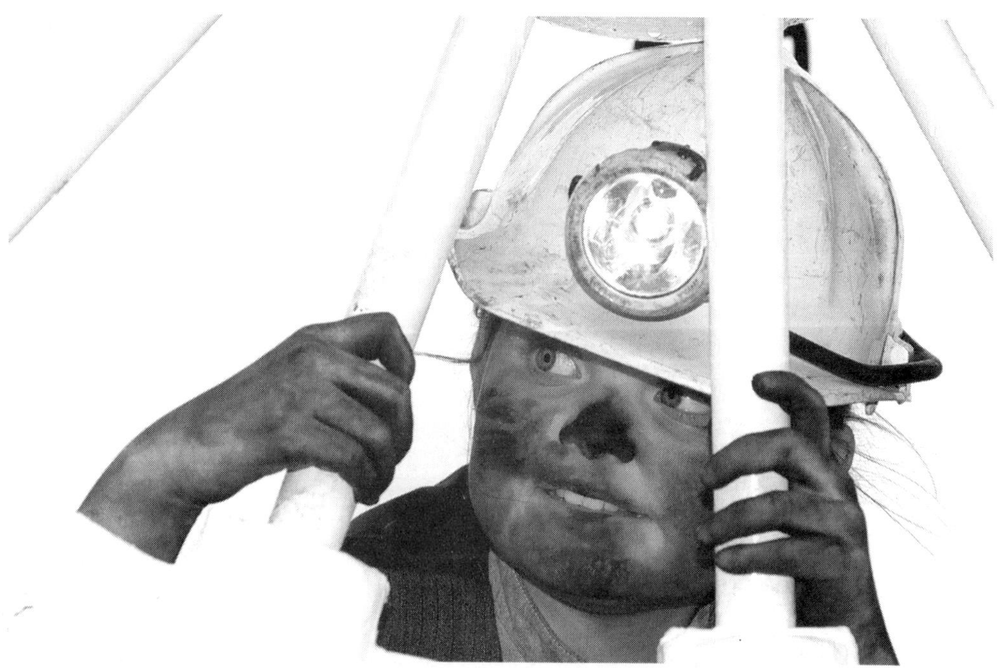

Bowes Railway Museum float in the Millennium parade. Since the closure of the local mines, Houghton Feast has become even more important as a community event.

Happy smiles from a float in the 1976 carnival parade.

The real Village People performing the YMCA song or Houghton village people providing fun and laughs at the 2000 carnival parade?

Aliens on a float at the carnival parade. One local resident recalls taking part in the outdoor community hymn singing with her mother and seeing three circular shaped objects in the sky.

Vintage bicycles from Beamish Museum are another regular sight at the carnival parade.

Young children showing community spirit on a float in the Millennium parade.

This float from the 2001 parade took the theme of Lewis Carroll's 'Alice Through the Looking Glass' stories. In 1998, the entire parade took the theme of book titles to mark the National Year of Reading.

The cover of the 1993 Houghton Feast programme of events.

"I have been closely involved with Houghton Rugby Club since 1948. For Houghton Feast, we ran a schoolboy competition for many years on Feast Saturday and also a Senior match v Sunderland Rugby Clubs on the Sunday."

Stuart McLaren, President of Houghton Rugby Club, 2002

CHAPTER 7

ILLUMINATIONS

A montage of illuminations with Annie Pratt, Mayor of Sunderland in 1983.

[Photograph: Northeast Press Ltd., Sunderland Echo]

A relaxing scene in the Rectory Park during the 1970s, with Feast illuminations in the background. In 1975, the range of illuminations was increased, with streetlights being introduced to Newbottle Street.

An illumination at night in the Rectory Park, during the 1970s.

Houghton Feast illuminations as seen in 1984. This particular piece was reused several times with the digits of the date being replaced each year.

A clown illumination piece with the old Rectory in the background.

Illuminations in the Rectory Park, viewed from the Broadway.

The Magic Roundabout illumination piece in the Rectory Park.

Mayor Annie Pratt with a Feast illumination piece in 1983. A lot of the illuminations were made by the Council's Engineering Department.

[Photograph: Northeast Press Ltd., Sunderland Echo]

The Broadway in 1973. The display behind the seated gentlemen is of Walt Disney's 'The Jungle Book'. Illuminations were added to Houghton Feast after World War II and mainly focused on St. Michael's Church. The lights were a welcome change from the blackouts of the war years.

CHAPTER 8

COMMUNITY HYMN SINGING

The visit of the Bishop of Durham, Rev Maurice Harland, and the presence of television cameras at the community hymn singing in 1965, led to an estimated crowd of eight thousand in the Broadway.

"In 1949, Rector Gwilliam proposed that, after Evensong on Feast Sunday, the congregation would sing hymns on the Broadway. We came out of Church to find the Broadway packed with people. As a fourteen year old, I helped to distribute hymn sheets among the crowds of people. They stood packed together and the buses could not get through. After 1949, choirs from other churches in Houghton, joined us in the outdoor hymn singing. It was the beginning of the revival of Houghton Feast."

Memories from Marion Toy, 1949

Houghton Feast Sunday, 1950. The Church was floodlit and the Evensong was relayed to the crowds in the Broadway, as shown here a year after the first outdoor hymn singing.

A view of the Broadway from the White Lion pub at the hymn singing in 1954.

Community hymn singing at Houghton Feast. Pictured are Rector Gwilliam, Councillor John Mawston and Thomas Urwin, M.P., *circa* 1967.

Local people taking part in the outdoor community hymn singing. The young girl to the left seems to be finding the songs on her hymn sheet rather tasty!

A view of the singing crowd in the Broadway.

"I remember going to Houghton Feast before I was married, in 1932. It was a treat and I have happy memories. I would walk there and back with school friends and stalls lined the Broadway in front of the Church. I remember a funny incident. At the Sunday evening hymn singing, a Mrs Turnbull was there wearing a hat made from feathers. A gale blew up just as the hymn was finishing and she said, 'I'll have to buy a hairnet to go over these feathers'. It went out over the loudspeaker and everyone in the Broadway heard! I can also remember charabancs coming from Shields, for day trips. Houghton was alive."

Memories from Elizabeth Porter,
Mayor of Sunderland 1975 - 1976
and former
Chairman of Houghton Urban District Council.

Children contributing to the community hymn singing in 1977.

"I remember the wonderful sound emanating from the various rides and trudging through the mud of the Lake in my wellies and riding the Shuggy Boats. I also remember the mystery of the sideshows that you never got in to see, the Saturday afternoon with your friends, riding the rides and eating candy floss, carefully counting your pennies to have enough left for your favourite ride. Who could forget the brawls afterwards, with the local teddy boys flexing their muscles? The best part was the excitement of the prelude to it all happening and the talk for days about the food you had and all the excitement of the weekend. At the Sunday night hymn singing, all the crowds were singing loud and clear and everybody was happy to be there even though it was a cold, damp night. As a policewoman, I remember standing in front of the Church with my hymn sheet, singing louder than those around me. It was the highlight of the Feast!"

Memories from Pat Crawford, 1960s

Five thousand hymn singers in the Broadway in 1962. The community hymn singing was often preceded by the blowing of a post horn from the Church tower by a Mr D. Hall.

A scene from the 1964 community hymn singing event, when over five thousand people took part.

Singing in the rain! Community hymn singing in 1963. The present day hymn singing now takes place inside the Church, owing to the usual bad weather in October.

More views of the hymn singing at Houghton Feast. Do any readers recognise any of the faces?

Choir singing at the community hymn singing event. In the past, the choir would often sing from the top of the Church tower.

Children from Houghton Secondary School singing in front of St. Michael's Church, as part of the community hymn singing.

More amazing scenes from the hymn singing in the Broadway.

A final glimpse of the community hymn singing scenes from the 1970s. It is hoped that the outdoor singing will return to Houghton Feast.

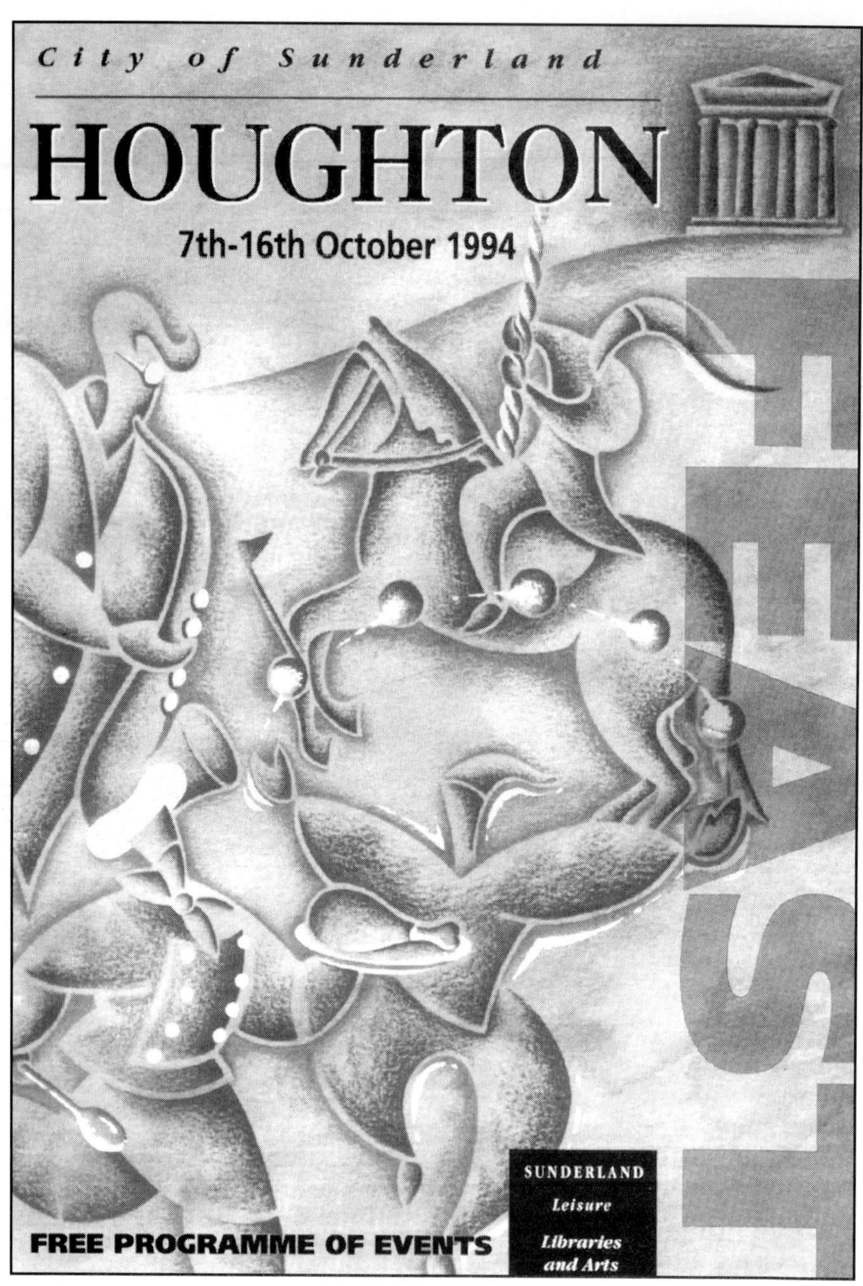

The cover of the 1994 Houghton Feast programme of events.

"I have ran the Houghton Feast Race several times. Last year I spoke to a woman competitor, an ex-pupil of Houghton Grammar School, who had lived for twenty years in America and returned to do the race! The race has had several versions with at least two routes, as traffic conditions have changed over the years."

Memory from Alan Purvis, 2002

CHAPTER 9

HOUGHTON FEAST RACES

A cycle race at Houghton Feast in the 1970s, with Elizabeth Porter presenting the trophy. In 1970, the winner of the Houghton Feast Cycle race was Eddie McGourley.

Racing of some form has always featured at Houghton Feast throughout the Festival's history.

Most people know of the horse, greyhound and cycle racing events but few are aware that in the mid 1800s ass racing, blindfolded wheelbarrow racing and racing on all fours were a common way of winning prizes of mutton, tobacco, alcohol and potatoes at Houghton Feast (see page 116). The races took place in Rectory Square (The Broadway) between the White Lion pub and the Red Lion pub.

The photographs in this chapter are a small glimpse into the diverse range of racing events held throughout Houghton over the Feast period.

A miners' day out at Houghton Feast races. The Feast was an authorised local holiday for miners until 1938.

Horse racing at Houghton Feast, October 13th, 1938, the last year it was featured at Houghton Feast.

Spectators at the Houghton Feast races in 1938. Horse racing was a major part of the Feast in the early part of the twentieth century. In The History & Antiquities of the County Palatine of Durham by William Fordyce it was said:

Houghton Feast is held annually on the Sunday after New Michaelmas Day, when the town becomes crowded with strangers at an early hour. The festival is continued for three or four days, during which there are horse-races and various other amusements, not only in the town, but in all the villages of the parish.

"As a child, I can always remember the sound of the horses' hooves at the Houghton Feast races."

Memory from A.C, 1930s

More spectators at the Houghton Feast races in 1938. The onset of World War II in 1939 was to see horse racing end and greyhound racing become more popular. During the War, entry was 1/3 for the paddock or 6d for the popular end. Admission was not permitted without a gas mask and uniformed members of His Majesty's Forces were given free entry.

The winners' enclosure at the Houghton Feast races in 1938. References to racing at Houghton Feast can be found as far back as 1825.

Police horses in the Broadway during Houghton Feast 2001. In pre-War years horse and carts were used to fetch visitors to the Feast from as far away as Sunderland and South Shields.

A pony taking a jump at the Houghton Feast Sports in 1949. Houghton Racecourse was also venue to foot running handicaps with prizes of £80 and £150.

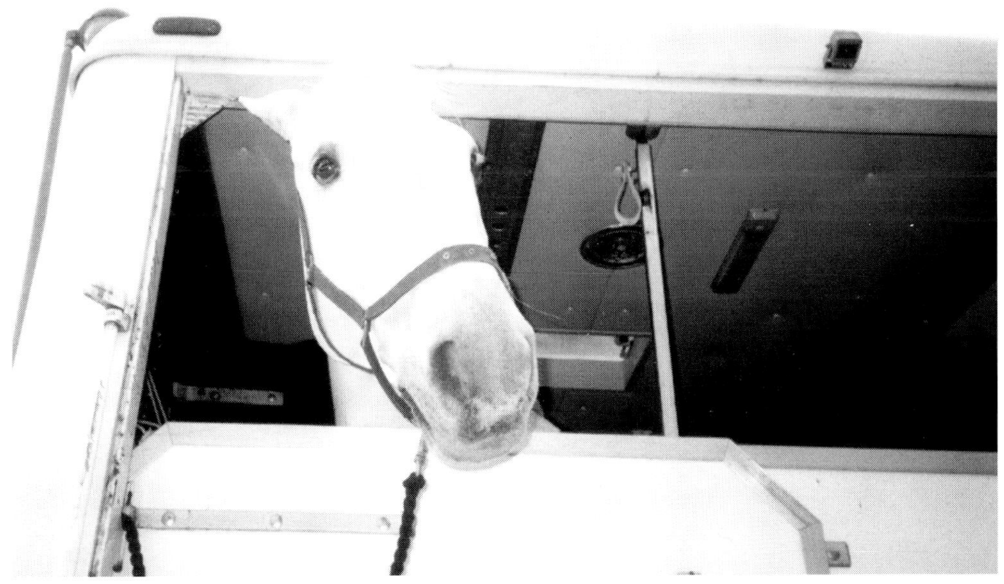

A police horse having a well deserved rest after patrolling the Broadway on carnival day 2001.

The Houghton Feast Greyhound Handicap on October 22nd, 1948. Hall Lane estate now occupies the site of the Greyhound Stadium.

Another greyhound racing in the Houghton Feast Greyhound Handicap, 1948. It was said in the 1946 Houghton-le-Spring Official Handbook that:

There is a Greyhound Stadium on the site of the old Race Course, which was actively associated with the historical Houghton Feast.

CHAPTER 10

MORE FUN AT THE FEAST

The photographs in this chapter cover the wide range of events and activities that has become familiar to the Feast programme over the years, including the Annual Cage Bird Exhibition, the Houghton Feast Horticultural Show, the well-loved Show Organs and the Pensioner's Tea Party.

The Annual Cage Bird Exhibition, above, is organised by the Hetton & Houghton Cage Bird Society and attracts a capacity audience to the Welfare Hall. Birds exhibited include Lovebirds, Australian Finches, Parrots, Canaries, Budgerigars and native British Finches.

"I visited about five years ago on a Saturday and had a ball. I particularly remember the wonderful street entertainment - stilt walkers, buskers, street theatre and fun fair."

Memory from Julia Hankin,
BBC Radio Newcastle, 2002

The Welfare Hall on Station Road is host to a range of Feast events, including this exhibition of exotic cage birds in 2000.

The annual Houghton Feast Horticultural Show, shown here in 2000, is housed in the Welfare Hall. The first open flower and vegetable show featured at the Feast in 1987.

An amazingly large cabbage at the annual Houghton Feast Horticultural Show. The total prize fund exceeds £3,000, with numerous trophies being presented to the various classes and sections.

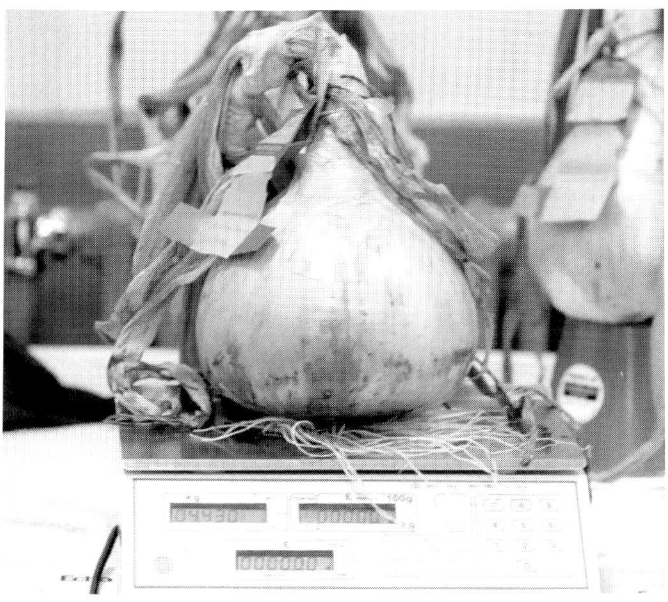

Another large vegetable in the Houghton Feast Horticultural Show. An auction of the produce sees the proceeds being donated to the Mayor of Sunderland's chosen charity.

Fairground organs were a popular feature at pre-War Feasts. It is said that they would play late into the night.

"In the early 1950s, George Parmley, Norman Smith, Alan Curry and myself restored and renovated a massive fairground organ - the mammoth Gaviolli Organ! It was 28ft long, 13ft 10in high and weighed almost 12 tons. Houghton District Council were very good, indeed. They paid us for bringing the organ to Houghton Feast. The organ is now always placed at the Feast to give the atmosphere of an old time fairground."

Memory from Billy Weeks, 1950s

The Gaviolli Organ in the grounds of the Council Offices, 2000.

Night time views of the organs from the previous page. In addition to the Show Organ Society of Great Britain's Gaviolli Organ, another three of the region's best organs were on display during the Millennium celebrations - the Gaviolli German Military 'Golden Ruth' Organ; the 65 Key Dutch Street Organ; and Wilf Husband's Dance Organ.

A rare view of the Houghton Feast pensioners' tea in the Welfare Hall, shown here in 1935.

A similar view in the Welfare Hall at the Houghton Feast Tea Dance in the year 2000.

The Houghton Feast pensioners' tea party, held in the Miner's Welfare Hall. The event proved popular when in 1961 over 650 pensioners attended.

Another view of the Houghton Feast pensioners' tea party in the 1960s. It was said that over 450 people attended the party and concert in 1964.

The cover of the 1996 Houghton Feast programme of events.

"After the Houghton Feast Church service, the chauffeur couldn't get the car door open. The last bus had gone and mobile phones weren't popular then. The chauffeur had to go and use the public phone whilst I waited outside with the very valuable Mayoral necklace!"

Memory from Annie Pratt,
Mayor of Sunderland 1983 - 1984

Chapter 11

HOUGHTON FEAST TIMELINE

"My grandmother, Mary Anne Robinson, had a shop in Fence Houses. She also had a stall at Houghton Feast on the corner of Church Street. She would sell ham and pease pudding sandwiches and her favourite saying was 'Mustard, hinny?' This was in the 1920s to 1930s."

Richard Curry, 2002

Left: Emily Lanagan with her three-year-old daughter, Linda, on the way to Houghton Feast in 1958. The large piece of paper in the child's hand is in fact a bus ticket.

1100s - Houghton Feast probably originated as Michaelmas - the festival of the dedication of the Parish Church of St. Michael and All Angels.

1517 - Bernard Gilpin was born.

1541 - Bernard Gilpin was ordained.

1557 - Bernard Gilpin became Rector of Houghton-le-Spring and helped expand the Michaelmas celebrations with his hospitality and the roasting of a bullock or hog.

1574 - Kepier Grammar School was founded by Bernard Gilpin and John Heath.

1583 - Bernard Gilpin was knocked down by an ox in Durham Market Place and died on March 4th.

"Houghton Feast makes this community. It is a good community celebration."

Dick Toy, 2002

HOUGHTON FEAST

" Sic transit gloria Houghtoni."

On Wednesday, the 8th day of October, 1845,
The following Prizes are to be contested for--

TO CLIMB A GREASY POLE,
For a *Leg of Mutton.*

A Boll of Potatoes
To be wheeled for, with wheelbarrows, blindfolded, from the White Lion to the Red Lion.

A Foot Race for a Hat,
Entries for the Hat at Mr. Thomas Steele's.

An Ass Race, For HALF A GUINEA.

A Race in Sacks,
FOR A SHOULDER OF MUTTON.

ANOTHER HAT TO BE RUN FOR,
The entries at Mr Christopher Harrison's.

One POUND of TOBACCO, to be Gurned for.

A QUANTITY OF ALE TO BE HOPPED FOR

A Race on all Fours, for a Gill of Rum.

And to conclude by singing the National Anthem in retiring to the respective Hotels to have the Prizes awarded.
The Amusements to take place in Rectory Square, Houghton, and to commence precisely at half-past two o'clock, when considerable sport is anticipated.

T. H. CURRY, AND G. FAIRBAIRN, ESQUIRES, STEWARDS.

VIVAT VICTORIA ET ALBERT.

Wright's "English Dialect Dictionary" gives 'gurn' or 'girm' as: "To show or gnash the teeth in rage or scorn; to snarl as a dog; to look savage; to distort the countenance; to speak in a snarling, surly tone" etc., and it describes 'girning-matches' as: "...used to be part of the local sports... the person who could girn to the judges satisfaction would get a quarter of a pound of tobacco as a prize. A horse-collar was used to girn through to add to the novelty"

A poster advertising Feast events in 1845.

1752 - The people of Houghton refused to accept the introduction of the Gregorian calendar and celebrated Michaelmas according to the Julian calendar on October 10, eleven days behind the Gregorian Calendar.

1784 - Billy Purvis, popular showman and entertainer, was born on January 13th, at Auchindinny, Scotland. The Purvis family moved to Newcastle two years later.

1818 - Billy Purvis visited Houghton Feast for the first time, and very probably set up his show booth in the Market Place.

1825 - Billy Purvis had a dispute with Dr Bell and Mr Myers over payment into a racing fund. At this time, racing was a popular feature at Houghton Feast.

"Houghton Feast continues to be a community focused celebration and because of the involvement of the local churches, children and young people are able to learn about the history of their locality."

Louise Farthing, 2002

A poster advertising Feast events in 1995 - exactly 150 years after the poster on the previous page.

1845 - Foot racing, blindfolded wheelbarrow racing, greasy pole climbing, ass racing, sack racing and a gurning competion featured at the Feast in Rectory Square (The Broadway). Prizes included a leg of mutton, a shoulder of mutton, a hat, a pound of tobacco, a quantity of ale and a gill of rum.

1848 - Peter Mackenzie, a well known Methodist preacher, visited Houghton Feast. Unfortunately, whilst he was visiting the fair, his bridle and saddle were stolen from his donkey and the animal had also rolled around in the mud, adding to his misery. On October 16th, Billy Purvis, with his show booth, made his thirtieth annual visit to the Feast.

1853 - On December 16th, Billy Purvis died and was buried at Saint Hilda's Church in Hartlepool.

Perzo the Clown from Scotland. The Sunshine Circus came to town in 2000 as part of the special Millennium celebrations.

1881 - Houghton Burn was diverted by Joseph Coulson to form a boating lake. Mill owners downstream were deprived of their water supply and started legal proceedings. The Lake was soon filled in by two Darlington showmen, the Robinson brothers, and used as a showground.

1887 - An ox was roasted in Houghton as part of the celebrations of Queen Victoria's Golden Jubilee.

1894 - The Houghton Urban District was formed.

1896 - An ox was roasted at the Lake grounds on New Year's Day. The animal was said to be a gift to the town from a showman who had visited the Feast.

1920s - John Murphy's grandfather made his first visit to Houghton Feast.

1930 - Confusion arose over whether Durham County Council or Houghton Urban District Council should receive the tolls collected from the erection of stalls in the Market Place.

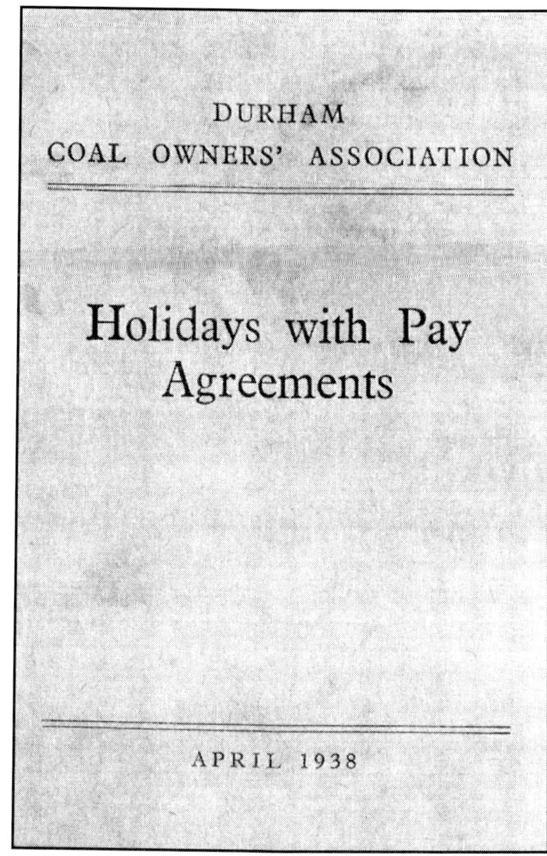
DURHAM
COAL OWNERS' ASSOCIATION
Holidays with Pay Agreements
APRIL 1938

"Houghton Feast is a boisterous reminder of Houghton's ancient and venerable past."

Ian Robinson, BBC Radio Newcastle, 2002

A miners' pay agreement booklet from 1938 stating:

The existing recognised public holidays shall not exceed eight, and the observance of local holidays, such as Race Week and Houghton Feast shall be discontinued.

1938 - Houghton Feast was no longer recognised as an official local holiday for miners. Horse racing was last featured at Houghton Feast in this year.

1939 & 1940 - The outbreak of World War II led to a reduction in Feast activities. Horse and foot racing discontinued, as did the fairground; however the greyhound racing and religious side of the Feast still went ahead.

1941 - The continuation of the War, lighting restrictions and transport difficulties meant that the fairground, again, was not featured at the Feast.

1942 - A parade of the Home Guards band, the Royal Tank Corps, police special constables, Civil Defence Forces, Army Cadets, Air Force Cadets, Girls Training Corps and Girl Guides took place on Feast Sunday. The choir also sang hymns from the tower of St. Michael's Church.

1943 & 1944 - Roundabouts and other amusements were featured at the Feast in the Market Place but the Lake grounds were left unused.

The Houghton Feast push-ball contest at Houghton Rugby Club in 1967, refereed by Councillor John Mawston. The contest was one of the extended events as part of the Houghton Feast revival and ended in a draw.

1945 - The fairgrounds returned to both sites - the Lake grounds and the Market Place. A military parade once again featured at the Feast, and Rev Oswald Noel Gwilliam, Vicar of Seaham, preached at the Church service. The effects of the War would have many implications on Houghton Feast for years to come.

1947 - Illuminations were introduced to Houghton Feast. The lights centred mainly on St. Michael's Church.

1948 - Oswald Noel Gwilliam became Rector of Houghton and helped rejuvenate the Feast celebrations. John Murphy made his first visit to the Lake fairground with the Waltzer.

1949 - Rector Gwilliam initiated the outdoor community hymn singing event and placed a greater emphasis on the religious aspects of the Feast.

1953 - The community hymn singing took place in the Broadway under an illuminated ERII emblem in the Queen's Coronation year.

"Houghton Feast was such an important event that my husband had to do school work related to it in class. Everyone looked forward to it."

Memory from Teresa Legg, 2002

Gary Gifford, street entertainer, in the grounds of Houghton Kepier School. Mr Gifford only allowed his photograph to be taken on the condition that the photographer would juggle fire with him!

1955 - John Mawston joined the Urban District Council.

1958 - All employees of the Urban District Council were granted a two day holiday with pay for Houghton Feast Monday and Tuesday.

1960 to 1963 - Owing to housing redevelopments, the Urban District Council decided not to use the Market Place for the fairground, using only the Lake grounds. It was also suggested that the Kirklea field be used instead.

1965 - The Bishop of Durham, Rev Harland, visited the community hymn singing, having first visited Houghton Feast in 1961. The additional presence of television cameras helped attract an estimated crowd of eight thousand people to the Broadway.

1967 - An important change took place in the organisation of the Feast. The Houghton Feast Steering Committee was formed and Houghton Rotary Club revived the tradition of ox roasting. The carnival parade and music festivals were also added to the Feast line-up. Houghton Feast was billed as 'new style, 1967'. This was the last year in which the fair was sited on the Lake and Market Place.

"The feast is a solid traditional community event."

Sally Mitten, 2002

The Houghton Feast fireworks are generously supported by the Showman's Guild of Great Britain (Northern Section) and are one of the three big events of modern day Houghton Feasts.

1968 - The Rectory field site was first used for the fairground and a Mr Jaconelli was given permission to sell ice cream there. Mr G. Freeman of Gateshead won the first Houghton Feast Whippet Racing handicap trophy. Major James Howe MBE, who was born at Penshaw, played at Houghton Feast with the Band of the Scots Guards.

1970s - A new bus station opened up on the Lake site. It was also in this decade that community hymn singing outside ended. Rector Gwilliam left the Parish in 1972.

1974 - The Feast began to be assisted by the resources of Sunderland Borough's Recreation Department on the reorganisation of Local Government.

The amazing fireworks display at Durham Road playing fields, on Feast Monday. In 1987, a fireworks display was held on Feast Friday as a grand finale to the opening ceremony.

1975 - The range of illuminations was extended, with streetlights being introduced to Newbottle Street. A marquee was erected in the Rectory Park to house a flower & vegetable show.

1976 - The night of the opening ceremony was changed from the usual Friday to Thursday to accommodate Mayor Charles Slater's Jewish faith.

1977 - The Queen's Silver Jubilee featured heavily in the Houghton Feast celebrations with red, white and blue Union flags adorning the parade floats.

1981 - Houghton-le-Spring Pipe Band first featured at Houghton Feast.

1982 - Extreme bad weather at the Feast led to talks of switching the fairground site from the Rectory field to the all-weather sports ground near Station Road.

1984 - John Price became the officer responsible for organising the Festival.

"Houghton Feast is a fun link with the past."
Jim Edger, 2002

Enjoying a nice cuppa at the Houghton Feast pensioners' tea party in the Welfare Hall, *circa* 1940.

1985 - The first Military Tattoo was included in the opening ceremony and featured the Light Infantry Band, North East Pipe Bands, South Shields Sea Cadets Band, Ryhope Colliery Welfare Band and the Claire McKenzie Dancers.

1987 - Councillor John Mawston, Chairman of the Houghton Feast Steering Committee, became Mayor of Sunderland. The first Houghton Feast Open Flower & Vegetable show was held in the Welfare Hall.

1993 - Illuminated features were re-introduced to the Rectory Park and the Feast took the theme of 'industrial heritage'.

1994 - The first Houghton Feast Family Fun Run featured at the Feast.

"I was involved with Houghton Feast in October 1993. Marilyn Hopkins and I, with various groups, produced a series of wall hangings in the weeks leading up to the Feast. The panels of the Houghton Textile depicted many scenes from around Houghton."

Jean Carverhill, 2002

Left: The Houghton Feast Tea Dance in the year 2000. The event is arranged by Houghton Age Concern and is traditionally held in the Welfare Hall.

1996 - The purpose-made ox roasting equipment disappeared and no ox roasting took place.

1997 - A memorial service was held in St. Michael's Church for Noel Gwilliam, who had died on February 21st. In October, a newly constructed ox roasting spit was unveiled. The illuminations were relaunched.

1998 - The first boneless ox roasting took place as new Government legislation banning beef on the bone was introduced. John Murphy made his fiftieth annual visit to the Feast and the Feast went online with CyberFest - a day of computer and Internet fun. A Houghton Feast website was also launched.

A side stall on the Rectory field fairground, 2000, with the Meteorite ride in the background.

"One memory of Houghton Feast that I will never forget is just before World War II. I was working as an usherette at the Coliseum Picture House. In the break between the first and second house film shows, my friend and I went across to the Feast activities. I went on the Shuggy Boats and loved it - but I was quite sick when I came off! I made my way back to the Coliseum only to be told by the very cross manager that I was late. He sacked me on the spot!"

Memory from Lily Anderson, 1930s

1999 - A side stall on the Rectory field fairground caught fire.

2000 - A Millennium beacon was ignited on the top of St. Michael's Church, as brand new Feast illuminations were unveiled.

2001 - Sunderland Mayor Ken Murray opened the Rectory field fairground early for specially invited children and unveiled the new tarmac pathways. The foot and mouth epidemic led to the traditional ox roast sandwiches increasing in cost and the Feast took the theme of 'celebration' to commemorate the regeneration of Houghton.

To be continued. . . .